the task of falling rain

poems

shirley a. plummer

©Shirley A. Plummer
All rights reserved.
ISBN-13: 978-0692509586
ISBN-10: 0692509585
Cover design by Chris Graamans
Turnstone colophon courtesy of Pepper Trail
Turnstone Books of Oregon, LLC
Seal Rock, OR

DEDICATION

To my lifelong friend Frieda May Carlson Nusom,
who wouldn't let me slip away.

To those most supportive of my fragile ego
and who contributed most to the growth and
development of my independence and creativity:
Michael Cunningham Kaye,
Jean Hobson Rich,
Joseph & Glendyne Wigley,
and especially my companion
of more than thirty years,
Frank Thomas Rafferty, M.D.

To writer friends:
Don Manker and Walter Stevens,
an'ya and Peter B.,
Drew Myron and Shirley Kishiyama;
Jean Esteve and Marianne Klekacz,
Dorothy Blackcrow, who first invited me to Tuesday,
and other members of Tuesday
especially my editors,
Ruth F. Harrison and Sandra Mason

IN MEMORIAM, FTR (1925-2006)

Oceans

what is soluble or separable enters the oceans
from a stream that empties into the sea
a lake, if lacking outlet
soaks into the earth
seeping through
emerging in rivulets
or evaporating into the sky
falling as rain on water
falling as rain on land

rainwashed dust and smoke,
even sand is moved by the sea
and the edge of one sea blends into the next

You, love, may be in the smoke, the mist
or all the seven seas
I, solidly grounded, weighted in place
look on the Pacific remembering

We are not so far apart perhaps
as you from this world
or I from where I left you last
slipping through my fingers
into the small stream   near the Atlantic

CONTENTS

the task of falling rain	1
early morning	2
bearing gifts	4
The Watcher	5
a moment	6
one thing	7
after rainstorms	8
winter ocean	9
west of the Coast Range	10
retreat	11
seasonal creek	12
my part of the Pacific	14
escape	16
ebb tide	18
NOW	19
Nightfall	20
On the Beach	22
Smooth Sea	23
by the sea	24
Windy day on the coast	25
wintery warnings	26
windstorm	28
amber autumn	30
living near a mountain	31
mayfly weather	32
re-moving	34
Watery lemon yellow sky	35
haunted by a strange sunset	36
Evening dusk	37
pastel sunset	38
winter sun	39
another quiet evening	40
Blues, a song with Ian C. Smith	41
hope	42
away from home	43

the sun, the rain, the holly tree	44
Portrait of a Morning:	
Stonefield Beach, mid-November	46
improbable truths	48
The Bat	49
NEWSFLASH	50
Island Life; seen out the kitchen window	51
empty sky	52
I captured a yellowthroat in my hands	53
rhododendron blossoms	54
eight orange tulips	55
young artist	56
behind the waterfall	57
the botanist	58
the spinner	59
the last fly	60
alone among strangers	61
too deep for tears	62
roots	63
Crops after Mining	64
news item:	65
coastal highway	66
the accident	67
almost an invitation	68
perspective	69
rest	70
walking in snowy fields	71
optical illusion	73
from the outer world	74
let it be summer	76
frost and cold	79
Reviews	80
About the author	82

LIST OF ILLUSTRATIONS

"To wash leaves," Chris Graamans, opposite 1

"Mist outlines each ridge," Rex A. Smith, 3

"For one large soaring bird," Ian C. Smith, 8

"Foggy Oregon Coast," Teresa Teet,
acrylic on canvas, 13

"Sun and shade," Ian C. Smith, 17

"No marks stay," Ian C. Smith, 22

"Sweetbriar," Shirley Plummer, 24

"Twigs and small branches," Chris Graamans, 29

"Sky reflected on the wet sand," Ian C. Smith, 35

"The many layers of clouds," Ian C. Smith, 40

"Until there is no time," Ian C. Smith, 62

"Optical illusion," Rex A. Smith, 72

"Leading to the world," Ian C. Smith, 75

"Icy beach," Rex A. Smith, 78

ACKNOWLEDGMENTS

Oceans first appeared in *Concord*, 4 (2012).

the task of falling rain, ebb tide (*To Find Peace*, revised), *by the sea*, and *re-moving* first appeared in *Tuesday*, 8 (2014).

Nightfall (revised) first appeared in *Tuesday*, 5 (2010-2011) and was recorded for Oregon Poetic Voices, #0203107 (30 August 2011) (as *Nightfall in the High Rockies*).

Portrait of a Morning: Stonefield Beach, mid-November first appeared as *Early morning sea report* in *Concord*, 6 (2014).

yellowthroat, first limited edition 1/1 to Paulann Petersen, "Rain on the River," paint on paper (24 April 2011).

the botanist, 1st and 2nd Honorable Mentions (Dueling Judges), Oregon Poetry Association, Spring, 2012 contest.

the spinner, 2nd Place, Northwest Poets' Concord contest, 2011. First appeared in *Concord*, 3 (2011) and was recorded for Oregon Poetic Voices, #0203107 (30 August 2011).

perspective, 1st Honorable Mention (New Poets), Oregon Poetry Association, Fall, 2011 contest.

the task of falling rain

to lay dust
    and wash leaves
to brighten blossoms
    and make the earth smell new
to cool a summer day
    and make a casual walk pleasant
to play a tune on the shimmering leaves
    a lullaby on a tent, a tattoo on a skylight

to allow one to feel again like a small child –
    tongue tasting rain – jumping on puddles

to mask and wash away gentle tears for
    long ago remembrances

early morning

Light morning mist outlines each ridge . . .
on the highest
trees espaliered against white cloud
flatten into silhouettes

We know each valley and small vale,
singly or together we have entered every one

following some 'til they join
little-used forest service roads
or tracks to an old trapper's camp,
even trails made by deer or elk

we have not yet exited every one
nor followed every fork

There is mystery
but no more than in other forests –
they all invite, each of them draws us to explore
and when the trail forks, whatever the choice,
the neglected one becomes the more appealing
the more mysterious . . .

but if we turn back
we neither discover the secrets of the first-chosen
nor find where it ends or emerges

We keep a diary to know each possibility probed
and those that have yet to be explored . . .
to find where the lion lives
and if the coyotes hang out in that cave

This morning I looked at trail maps
and waited for a weather change . . .
no path is chosen for today

I watched for the mist to dissipate
but now it rains . . .
each ridge becomes more veiled until
the farthest is a faint smudge

bearing gifts

backed against the forest of spruce
on the downhill side of the Coast Range
nearly to the sea – the cabin
is embedded in windless quiet –

but listen, the oncoming wind
like a train roaring
through the treetops
brings spendthrift rain

rain to rattle the roof
rain to batter early azaleas
rain to drench the walker caught out –

lavish rain restores the small creek's rush
that now sets the one-stone dam
sparkling and spilling over

The Watcher

Fog gathers until all blue
disappears from the still-bright sky
The watcher sits in a patch of veiled sun

and imagines a valley filled
with mist rising from a river
hiding farther trees and hills

Fog threads through
mixed woods   then spruce
making grey ghosts of trees

but in the small clearing
the watcher waits
and imagines an ocean obscured
by fog   moving in   over the land
the road   the field   the hedgerow . . .

A hazy spot past the zenith
shows the sun   obscured
is still there

Thickening fog hushes sound
Lessening light drains color
The watcher shivers

and imagines a paler planet
It is a darkling hour and cooling

a moment

low clouds blown swiftly southward
though light and fluffy
dim the afternoon sunlight

the sudden change in brightness
cools the air

one thing

enticed out by mild sunshine
this spring has much the same as last . . .
early bulbs, forsythia, flowering quince
redbud blooming on trunks and bare branches
the marsh stained with purple blossoms

and many more renewals of life . . .
compelled to omit a pleasure each year
'til all were gone but one . . .
I would wish kept back
the only one now missing

you have left . . .
nothing else matters

after rainstorms

walking on Stonefield Beach
after rainstorms

small streams seep
    through cliffs and banks to the sea
carry the smell of forest deaths . . .
    rotten leaves, fallen wood,
    animals whose span is done . . .
dust to dust and around again

the solute filtered through humus and soil
runs over and around roots and rocks
staining the sand to the sea

winter ocean

Stonefield beach provides a daily panorama
of sand and sea and sky
each very like the one before but not quite,
widths, textures, and layers varying
colors shifting shades, of blue, white, slate

long banks of clouds reach side to side
long ranks of waves pour over mostly hidden beach
soon to be revealed as the tide turns
and lessening waves hiss over stretches of sand

today the entire view is horizontal
and the light is exactly right
to make a Japanese-print sea
the dark strip of that peculiar blue
from the horizon shading
lighter toward the beach –

the sun breaks through and lays
a sliver of silver along the horizon
the shadow of a long cloud paints
a dull strip on the sea
then a broader, bright reflection
fades forward to no color at all

to complete the picture
a distant black tick mark –
for one large soaring bird

west of the Coast Range

heavy, dark storm clouds
gravid with rain withheld
shadow the draining gullies
and blacken the river

too clumsy to rise over
the cloud stumbles into the ridges –
belly rips open to deliver
drenching rain on the mountain

the clouds lighten, rise
and shred over the peaks
to scatter white froth in the blue sky
covering the sun-filled valley beyond

retreat

my cabin is in the woods
next the Siuslaw Forest;
higher up the mountain are space to write
and windows to watch the sea

but not high enough to see Tenmile Creek . . .
I can tell where it is . . . between the marsh grass
and the sandspit that turns it north
before it curves again into the Pacific

sometimes the creek is traced
by birds following it upstream
marbled murrelets busily carry food
to nestlings miles back in the woods

swallows and swifts skim for insects
noisy kingfishers dive for small fish
gulls like clumsy flycatchers feed greedily
when there is a hatch of flying ants

the sandspit collects driftwood
which winter storms remove, throw high
on bluffs, fling down on other beaches,
and deposit different pieces in their place

soon I will again search out
branches for walking sticks
and a fence, and worn planks
for a shed by the cabin

seasonal creek

the small seasonal creek
that runs under the foot bridge
did not dry up in this short summer
the tiny waterfall splashes still

upstream from the bridge
through thick undergrowth
the creek emerges from national forest
into an idea of a meadow, then narrows
as old Sitka crowd back on either side . . .

a tiny ravine guides the water
between large roots of standing trees
and fallen spruce
to a single, wedged rock . . .
a dam over which the creek
spills before it spreads

it makes a minuscule marsh
there and under the bridge
for water hemlock, skunk cabbage
and a muddy edge
where animal tracks collect

below the bridge broad leaves give way to sedges,
the stream divides making a doll-size island
one channel washes the rock-lined bank
close to the end of the cabin
near a section of old Highway 101

the channels come together
through sedge, fuchsia, wild carrot
then flow beneath a low-hung pine branch
back into thick undergrowth
and vanish under the old road

my part of the Pacific

comes to me on a long sandy beach
ending in rocky opportunities for splash and crash
at either end under small bluffs,
each the end of a mountain ridge
south, too far for sound to reach my ears
north, nearly opposite but the bluff blocks the sound
~   ~   ~
the sea is always in my senses:

the sound, not of the breakers that thin at my feet
or the clatter of shell and pebble in the wave
    drawing back from a steep beach
but the low underlying roar
best heard in the otherwise silent night

the smell of ozone
    forgotten until a storm makes it again detectable
and the other smell of rain
    filtered through forest floor and clay bank
    following its stained trickle to the sea

to taste and feel I go to the beach – not often now
    my son brings me rocks still wet:
    I detect the slippery and
        salty nature of the sea on them

and the sight, always outside the window,
is visible most nights by moon- and star- light
or lacking those, the lights of fishing boats
performing their sentry duty
across and back before the horizon
~   ~   ~

though raised in the valley this is where I feel home

as an eskimo, to die peacefully,
without burden to family and tribe,
walked or was carried to an ice floe
I should disappear from all knowledge of my ending

in time I should like to walk into my part of the sea

escape

> "Children, like animals, use all their senses
> to discover the world." –Eudora Welty

racing over fields to get into the trees
loping through woods
as an escaping prisoner might
to get away, he from pursuit,
I from people, noise, demands

the sun shining through vine maple leaves

I look at every thing –
patterns on bark mimic a wave settling into the sand
    and sliding under the outgoing tide,
    clouds make faces and other forms,
    still other shapes are drawn in forest litter;
various mosses grow on logs –
    one looks like a minuscule
    forest of palm trees;
a narrow, quarter-inch long black beetle struggles
    through the lush growth between 'palms';
a foot away the 'trees' are different
and there are tiny mushrooms
and stems with grey cups atop filled with
    reddish grains of pollen

on a larger scale there are trillium, wild iris,
    yellow wood violets, white candytufts
on lucky days, in shadier, moister spots,
    I find Indian pipes – not flowers at all,
    those translucent, white saprophytes –
    yet lovelier than many flowers,
    though in a funereal sort of way

and as my luck holds, in a sunny spot
    bright pink shooting stars;
then a patch of oxalis leaves to chew –
    the slight lemon bite on my tongue
    cool juice running down my throat

I like the early light-green,
    the flowers smaller than a pencil round,
    more brazen flowers too,
    the heather's dark shiny leaves

I like the colors, aromas, tastes
    the stipple of sun and shade –
all add to the calm, nothing ruffles the serenity
of an escapee who sought refuge here

ebb tide

each day
I watch one
diminishing wave
slip under the next
it draws me out
to the center
of light

unsure
out or in
or dissolved
in the expanse
I search
I seek

NOW

                      now is fleeting

        cease grieving the past
lost love, lost health, lost time

        seek joy and beauty fresh
find friends, new poems, new flowers

        here now, now gone

                    touch more softly
all things beloved
                    listen more carefully . . .
that rustle of leaves
                    drink more deeply
of cold springs and wild violet scent

        now is fleeting

                  look more closely . . .
magnified in that dewdrop . . .

                now is fleeting

Nightfall

I. in the high Rockies

angle and a trick of light
enlarge the setting sun
a twenty-dollar gold piece
sitting atop a near peak

the sun drops behind
and all light falls with it
like a sheet pulled
by a sleeper falling out of bed

the temperature too drops –
in another part of the sky
the shivery, pale moon appears

II. near a large body of water

night falls gently on a western shore
even after the sun slips away
behind the sea it long
continues to light the sky

the dark creeps up from the east
easing the light around
to the other side of the world
for morning in another place

high clouds still alight
blue sky showing around –
clouds nearer the sea darken
as a mind loses light on its way to ground

III. the choice

nightfall in the mountains
is abrupt – harsh
as a meteor strikes, spreads a pall
blots out everything

I choose to live with the sea
I would prefer to die with the light
as night masks high valleys
and my sight

On the Beach

Rare windless day
sitting at sea level
watching waves
thinking on good and evil

Sitting at sea level
the ocean looms
innocent of intent, be mindful
it proffers doom

The ocean looms
out and in, slow motion
hissing sand whispers doom
and sweeps into the ocean

Slowly out and in
no marks stay
all swept into the ocean
on a rare windless day

Smooth Sea

I walk the beach seeking solutions
to seemingly impenetrable problems
An idea under that large clam shell?
a clue in that closed mussel?

Who knows what might be amidst
the litter left by the highest wave –
all those bits and pieces
thick with dancing sand fleas
jumping, jumping as if on a hot griddle

Today the sea is almost without waves
One turns over, shows its petticoats,
creeps ashore, and thins in the sand
The edge disappears as raindrops on dry crops
and the rest eases back under the next wave

Watching the sea
brings calm and tranquility
smooths turbulent thoughts
and answers begin to appear

by the sea

an hour of fading light remains
of this summer night, and the sweetbriar,
the eglantine of Shakespeare,
has furled its flowers

these long, light evenings pay
reparations for short, dark days
that make us wish to den with the bears
when wild storms blow danger

Windy day on the coast

The wind whips branches,
whines into the sunporch
blowing open the door

Except for the Umbrella Drill Team
in the Yachats* Fourth of July parade,
an open umbrella is rarely seen

Like a boat turned into the wind
to allow sail handling
cars must be parked into the wind

for doors chance being torn off
or bent out of usefulness –
like inside-out umbrellas

*yah'-hots

wintery warnings

some chill mornings and storms interrupt summer
yet after yesterday's wind and drenching downpour
the afternoon promised calm and sunshine

and so it was – but last night after dark,
our post-dinner game with the family from uphill
stopped when a power outage left us in the dark

without wind, without a sound

not even a moon,
not even the sea reflecting ambient light
lessened a more absolute lack than was usual

       ~   ~   ~

    scurrying like mice in the darkness
    everyone scrambled for flashlights
    or fumbled for the old phone
    that works on land lines
    (unless they too were broken)
    or switched off whatever had been on

    the only electricity remaining
    an intermittent red flash and buzz
    from the backup under my desk
    warning that the computer was on battery

    the three walked uphill to their own dark house,
    we did what clearing up we could then sat
    where we had been, reading with flashlights
    a camp light, my grandson's headlamp –

      soon we took our books and lights
      to burrow in our own beds

~   ~   ~

power was restored during the night
and I wakened to the one light left on

now I am drinking tea at seven o'clock
in the dark of a cold morning
winter-like even before summer is through

the morning is dark and still, but it promises
another calm and sunny day

windstorm

the wind whips leaves early to the ground
streets of red, sidewalks of gold,

brick walls retain green lawns
littered with yellow leaves,
twigs and small branches add to the clutter

large branches and whole trees
fall across sidewalks and streets
stopping traffic faster than a red light ever did

amber autumn

Amber paints the autumn
shades and variations
red-orange yellow brown
still it is singularly amber

Sound too is singular –
across the range of strike and speed
sharp and dull
ground squirrel's chitter insects' churr
    all combined mask the sound of the snake
    hidden under the bush
    that rattles its seeds,
    loose inside dry pods,
    in the lightest of winds

The cacophony blends to a steady, rough hum
The wave lengths of light and sound
    may have joined together
What sense perceives
    the blended colors sounds touches
    or the overlapping of aroma and taste?

Leaves thick on the ground disguise the sidewalk
and if you are charmed and walk by the right tree
you step regally on red carpet

Yesterday blossoms on the blackberry
    now only berries – green white dark red
    and leaves – turning yellow
Today the aroma of ripe berries warmed by the sun
    flavors the air

living near a mountain

I stand close on the west side of the mountain
the risen sun strikes my surroundings
       hit or miss – there but not here . . .

in reverse order of the sun's direction
it first lights the sea, and then the shore
       crosses the highway, then the front field . . .

already touching the mountain south of the creek
       from my still shaded place . . .
rising higher the light approaches me

I await the warmth of day . . .
the autumn chill even cooler on my skin
here in the shade

mayfly weather

> "It's summer before the grass grows,
> Not yet autumn when the leaves fall."
> –*Words from Cold Mountain*, Han Shan

decades ago in a ravaged Korea
bare of the plant life that would clue the season,
deserted paddies and leveled cities
showed only dirty snow or brown rubble
but on a hillside, lacking any touch of green,
shrubby sticks carried,
spaced along their branches,
palest possible lavender … pale almost to white …
wild azalea blossoms

ten years later in Montana
my pristine white 'Easter Lily'
bloomed one day and died the next,
destroyed in mid-July
by the last snow of the winter

the following year
I gathered our entire tomato crop, green
in mid-August to avoid its destruction
by the first snow of the year

much later, spending holidays in Oregon,
I wore a short-sleeved shirt and pedal pushers
to the garden on New Year's Day
to pull carrots for appetizers
before the big family dinner

now on the Oregon coast,
almost Thanksgiving Day:

    beside the new Stonefield house
    one red flower appears,
    accidentally seeded at the removal
    of earlier spent plants from
    the scarlet sea of summer poppies

    a few red azalea blooms show by the barn

    and fifteen miles north, up Highway 101
    one white azalea blossom opens outside
    the back door of St. Luke's-by-the-Sea

all risk sudden death-by-winter
to live ill-timed lives
led astray by errant weather

re-moving

reluctant to move yet again
even to escape the bone-chilling damp cold

I am preserved from thinking often of moving
by the sneak faux summer days
scattered throughout the winter
like broken sunlight glittering on the sea

Watery lemon yellow sky

Watery lemon yellow sky,
smoky cloud bank at the horizon
meets the dark grey-blue sea

Just past that last small wave
that creeps up the beach,
the sky is reflected
pale yellow on the wet sand

haunted by a strange sunset

I walk out of the woods
to watch the sun lowering

the strange, pale sunset haunts me
and I respond to the awful unreality
with visions – of burning bushes, salt pillars,
an empty crypt, a dead man speaking –

with a shiver I turn back to the trees –
as always the appeasing of the forest
restores my sense

Evening dusk

So much sea to reflect back
to the ever varying clouds
light from the sun long gone

No sunset colors in the sky
but miles from shore,
under the high white clouds
decklights,
bright as headlights in the night,
show where two fishing boats
follow their prey

pastel sunset

high clouds' undersides,
though lighted by the sun,
almost colorless – near cream

sun setting early behind a broad band
of distant clouds on the horizon

a few streaks of robin's-egg blue to the south
an expanse of blue to the north
the brightest color   but it too is pale

the sky   the clouds   the sun   the sea
all so muted   almost grey and white

I shiver in the sunlight
as a pale moon descends

winter sun

the pale, watery, winter sun finally
strikes the ground around the house,
on the front field, and across Highway 101
on the strip of public land
by Tenmile Creek and the sea

the sun's winter-late appearance –
delayed still more by clouds
hung over all week
as if drunk from
last week's sunny day –

obtrudes a bit of summer into winter –
it gives a foretaste of sunny days to come
and consolation for the gloom and grey,
but more comfort is found in remembering
the still-hidden Spring is storing up all this rain

another quiet evening

the many layers of clouds
varying from cream to peach
separated by strips of bright, clear blue

the tall bank of fog in the distance
does not prevent the sunset from turning fiery

**Blues, a song
with Ian C. Smith**

Of sky and water and forget-me-nots
I am the blue
of pale violets, feathers of a jay, and ice
I am the blue

of lapis and opal and hydrangea
I am the blue
of ribbons, velvet and old suede shoes
I am the blue

of satin-clothed boys and shepherds with horns
I am the blue
of extra moons and sapphires of dawn
I am the blue

of people suffering
I am the blue
but they would not have me disappear –
not from summer's noon

hope

I cannot find cupboard, closet, or cave
where my muse goes to rest

lying on the sand pondering
where I might find her

I leave my bones on the beach
with those of sea lions and gulls

the tide
slides . . . covers me
with detritus, driftwood and sand

the tide runs out
carrying much that it brought
leaving me laid on a half-buried tree

It is a treacherous beach that no muse visits
when a storm is imminent,
Perhaps with the next seventh wave . . .

The high wave that takes me
delivers, by the creek that leaves the land just there,
a manatee on a field of stones

away from home

the girl walked into the woods
again at home in the mossy seat
at the base of the Douglas fir found
her first summer in the Cascades

often she sat there, back leant against the trunk
whose big roots protected her on either side,
she thirstily drank in serenity – watched and
listened to small things in moss and grass

to birds in air and undergrowth
where animals moved, mostly unseen
but a gift if they came upon her unaware
and sometimes saw her and carried on

she rose early to walk in the forest
for at that hour it was all hers along with
the creatures whose lives were lived there,
for that time she was of them

later, the whole camp awake,
the giggly girls shouted and blundered
about frightening birds into hiding –
deer seldom appeared then

now an old woman enters refuges
finds a mossy seat, ground or log –
a mantle of contentment settles on her
and the dusk of evening descends

the sun, the rain, the holly tree

the view from my window
records changes in the light,
in the sun or rain, the clouds
    ~   ~

  a broader view would present more –
    hovering, diving, skimming seabirds
    seals and whales, each feeding in its fashion
other searchers over the sea in helicopters
fishing boats dithered over by gulls

  residents going east or west
    to seek food or head home to roost,
    in spring making many trips
    to feed nestlings

  passages of birds in great numbers
    tourists, and again the whales
    north or south by the season

  over the land eagles, hawks, ravens, crows
    all hunting . . . snakes, frogs, small mammals
    also hunting
songbirds eating insects and seeds
hummingbirds in swooping courtship
    or drinking flowers' nectar

  the holly berries reappear
    in the tree picked clean of red
    by marauding robins last spring
    ~   ~
I sometimes sit in the next room
    to oversee the full stage –
the ongoing procession

a few feet from my window
the holly tree blocks much of the view
and I can see only these few things
    the sun, the rain, the holly tree

Portrait of a Morning:
Stonefield Beach, mid-November

Rough, steel-grey sea
at high tide
breakers hide the beach
foam covers half the sea —
in the distance ghostly rollers break

the ground still shadowed
under grey clouds –
sky over the sea lightens
and far to the west a small patch
of blue appears

~ ~

The wind agitates the cypress tree
which sends different messages
from its various faces –
west, north, east:

    frenetic limbs beckon
    come in from the sea, come in from the sea

    others would brush one aside
    like a paddle pushing water back

    and opposite the ocean,
    they gently gesture, palm down
    be calm, it will change

And it does — abruptly
the wind stops

~ ~

the light increases
still the sun does not show
over the Coast Range
nor does it touch directly
anything visible
                      except —
those few distant cloud tops
white against the blue sky

improbable truths

after feeding in the shallows
a great white heron lifts its heavy body
the awkward rise followed by flight
of seemingly effortless grace

the dipper wades into bubbling creeks
    feeding on the pebbly bottom
continues walking and feeding
    even when submerged

pigeon-toed penguins
rocking their way to the sea
transform under water
into swift fliers
making quick changes of direction
darting after their food

a brown pelican barely skims the waves –
    rarely touching wingtip to water
    plashing with a turning wave –
flies high to watch for swimming shadows in the sea
dives arrow-swift then gracelessly crumples
    and the crash makes such a splash
    that he can't be seen –
    not diving into the water
    but sitting upon it –
as he pulls his bill up with its large pouch full of fish

always watching
another year should reveal more
fascinations

The Bat
    (for Tim Pfau)

I have worked to keep most of the wildlife
out of my log cabin
I have caught many mice and a few rats,
I have rescued birds and butterflies and bees,
snakes and slimy salamanders,
and even outdoor spiders
and a few insects

I have always welcomed the bats –
they dealt with biting insects for me . . .
at least our interests coincided

They could find their way in
and I opened the door for them
when they wanted to go out –

Even the one trapped while I was away
helped when he died.

He inurned himself in a wastebasket.

NEWSFLASH

Unseen here for thirty years.

Western bluebirds were reported
yesterday on Cape Perpetua.
Residents hope it is a second group.

Ten days ago a flock of bluebirds
were observed cavorting
around a house at Tenmile.

Island Life; seen out the kitchen window

On the lawn near the tidal ditch
the bluejay, belly to the ground
struggles against the kestrel
who like a lover, his body shadowing
the body beneath, presses
outspread wings that trace those
of the bird he forces down

Resistance ends …
the kestrel moves his catch
a short way to better cover

Some moviemakers, to evade the censors,
show a hand wielding a knife
striking down, and down again
at a target out of view

The feeding hawk's hooked beak
moves down and down
and up again with bits of flesh
torn from his prize
now hidden in the taller grass

empty sky

I once knew a man
who thought the most beautiful sky
was cloudless . . . empty blue
I shouldn't like to forgo the clouds . . .

or birds in the sky . . .
I taught him to like birds
caught him with the vision
of a scarlet tanager

yet I believe he died still thinking
a cloudless sky was best

I captured a yellowthroat in my hands

I captured a yellowthroat in my hands
my hands! – one under, one over
contained him while he calmed

outside, the covering hand lifted,
he sat in my palm
a few
      breathless
              moments

rhododendron blossoms

like the thistle,
with its multitude of tiny tubes
each with a drop of sweetness
only available to very long tongues,
the white rhododendron

as like as 'one' can be with 'many,'
litters the ground
with its single, circular petals
slipped from stamen and pistil
looking like handleless candle snuffers

perhaps the fairies were celebrating
until someone ceased believing
and they puffed into dusty air
leaving their pointed caps behind

eight orange tulips

drops of dew glint
on eight orange tulips
in a pot outside the door

last week
they looked to be destroyed
by the rain and wind –

they will open later today and
next week they will be gone

dewdrops sparkle in the sunlight

young artist

rectangular, plastic tub
yesterday filled with dirt
turned by overnight rain to mud

both hands slowly smoothing –
a sculptor caressing clay over a recumbent figure
down rib cage – dipping at the waist – slipping
over hip bone – down thigh

two small hands patting – petting
slowly stroking – smoothing –
a three-year-old neighbor
experiencing mud in a dishpan

behind the waterfall

the tallest of the falls on Silver Creek
in the Cascades
has a well-worn path running
behind the falling water

as a child I often walked there
to feel safe – hidden, and therefore, safe –
to peer out from the shallow cave
through the screen of water
at the less adventurous on the trail below

I felt safe even though
a careless step meant likely death . . .
I was sure-footed and seldom careless
and that was not what I feared . . .

still, death was a possibility
from striking rocks as I fell
from suffocating under the force of falling water
from drowning in the deep pool
gouged out by the continuous falls

but the beauty of the place is magnificent,
and dying is only dying

the botanist

the botanist concentrates,
searches out plant invaders
on low river banks and mud flats,
careful of boot-sucking mud

unaware of the turncoat trees
    releasing their wealth
    of bronze, copper, gold,
or the taste of salt from the sea

until, raising her head
in the cool of the evening
to hear –
    echoes of coyotes from upriver,
to savor –
    the aroma of burning wood,
to see –
    the first pale star

she turns homeward
with the taste of salt on her tongue
and a handful of leaves

the spinner

wool roving
ready for the distaff
has escaped the wheel –
it drapes on the headland,
tresses trail back toward the wind
blown from the sea

thin threads self-weave
on the warp of hillside spruce,
thicker threads hover the creek
and each small stream
that's open to sky and wind

reaching
to capture some
for your own wheel,
the warmth of your hand
dissipates
fog

the last fly

the fisher approaches the stream
that has provided decades of meals

she hears rather than sees
red-winged blackbirds …
their sweet voices in the cattails

a little downstream
a crow rasps in a near tree –

stepping into the shallows
she casts up past the small bend
where a German Brown takes the floating fly

the old leader snaps …fish and fly are gone
and the crow had flown with the cast

I must tie more flies for tomorrow

now a raven watches the fisher tie on
her last fly and flick it over the water

three black vultures approach
as she hooks another big trout

we have a fish for dinner

the raven cawing takes off down river
she turns to watch, leans as if to follow …

and with a small smile, falls face-down
unaware of the water closing over her …
or the soothing voices of redwings

alone among strangers

she went for a walk in the neighborhood
but parts of it seemed different . . .
not as they were yesterday

returning, she fumbles at the lock, not surprised
when the door is opened by a strange woman
who offers to take her home

three houses away the lock accepts her key
and the strange woman asks if she can call someone,
help her with anything – *No, . . . Yes . . .*

the bottled drinks in the refrigerator . . .
I can have one of those . . . I can't remove the cap
. . . I like the red ones

the strange woman searches the kitchen
but fails to find an opener, and,
reluctantly, leaves her alone . . .

it seems that she is nearly always alone now
strangers do help, or try
the pushier ones say they are her family . . .

she does not believe them

too deep for tears

> ". . . nothing can bring back the hour
> Of splendour in the grass, of glory in the flower. . . "
> —Wordsworth

I can't believe in eternity –
there is a limit to the hours
and those who thoughtless waste
are in possession of the powers
to make the world un-be

with wrong reason and no rhyme
destroying beauty, beast and past –
nothing now recall –
only standing, stunned   will last
until there is no time

so while I may not stay to see
the death of ev'rything I love
the child, the earth, the skies above –
it is not waste to watch the sea

roots

taproots thrust deep,
major side roots spread, dividing
into dendritic patterns
that reach the rainshadow edge where
the tree's umbrella of branches and leaves
guides rainwater to the dripline

roots send nutrient moisture back and up
feed needle and cone, leaf and seed
to increase the height of the tree
to add to the annual rings,
to thicken and lengthen roots
and add to their thirsty outward reaching

the cycle continues until age or disease
fells the giant,
if man has not already done so

Crops after Mining

>after reading
>*The Coach of Death* by William Blake:
>"parting is hard and death is terrible"

a creek empties *B Lake*, a poisonous remnant,
at a *parting* in the course
some *is* diverted
to irrigate *hard*, baked earth
it brings evil, *and* new shoots shrivel
only *death* comes
tainted soil *is* good for nothing
the water feeds a *terrible* crop of twisted weeds

news item:

"Smelt Sands, the small, innocent-looking cove
where two high school boys were washed away . . . "
not victims of the sea which just is
but of carelessness . . . ignorance . . . and perhaps
of that adolescent sense of immortality

the sea tosses half-ton logs high on bluffs;
it sweeps the unwary out to sea

coastal highway

she felt confined, as in a coffin
hurtling down the narrow road
in afternoon darkness of overcast
under constant, thin rain on soaked landscape

and on the windshield
heavy splatters from oncoming cars
blinding sheets of water from semis speeding by

and then the sharp turn around the cape
nothing ahead but sky and
sky – and then
sea

the accident

the road still shows signs
of last week's accident –
a bad one it was
. . . numerous emergency vehicles
roaring in, sirens blaring

no one left in a hurry

. . . many helpers straggled
into the little wood
between the highway and the sea
they returned slowly
wiping their mouths
taking shallow breaths

no one left in a hurry

even ambulances did not
rush away – did not
bother their sirens

. . . not washed soon enough
or well enough, the road
was left to erode away
the crassament – only
remaining evidence
of an accident
now faded to brown

no one stops
no one hurries by

almost an invitation

in youth, upon the approach
of one's true love,
there is a tickling of pleasure
and excitement
that bubbles up from the solar plexus
flutters under the diaphragm
through the chest and throat
and bursts into the flower of a smile

now it returns with a gasp
when driving the mountain road
hugging around Cape Perpetua
suddenly nothing ahead but sky –
and a far stretch of sea appears

perspective

in the high desert's cold air,
under sun blazing through thin air
a man's brain dizzies in its box,
his body evaporates into the dry air

a man knows
ice and fire of the past
made the fields of lava
and left ice caves
he now uses to cool his lunch

cold, thin, dry air
vast rock fields without visible life –
where he is bitten by insects or dry frost,
he sweats in enervating tropics,
he shivers in harsh polar air

a man is drawn to difficult, primitive places
perhaps to be reminded of the impersonal
nature of nature,
of the insignificance of his blot
on the planet,

perhaps to bring home
a thought-provoking memento –
a rock with a conchoidal fracture
and an edge
sharper than a surgeon's scalpel

rest

the day is done
the evening rose
reflects upon the sea

the cloud above
grows grey and more
it darkens as it soars

'til all light goes
and dark does rise
to cloak us to the close

but first stars light
and then the moon
to show us home the night

and when the dawn
returns too soon
we rise to work again

walking in snowy fields

I climb the hill to a fence –
an endless fence
no buildings in sight –
a single horse, shaggy in winter coat,
wanders over

I cannot reach hip or shoulder to pat
or even ear to scratch and,
not expecting to meet her,
I brought nothing –
no apple or carrot or sugar cube –

stroking her nose, I talk with her
listening to whinnied replies –

the increasing chill of late afternoon
creeps into my bones

reluctantly
I leave her standing by the fence –
she has nowhere to go
only back up the hill,
bare of all but grass and snow,
and out of sight, to whatever might be there

We seek what comfort we can and
I contemplate the value of companionship

The snow has stopped
I walk the grassy fields
bare of trees and houses

optical illusion

the light slants upward
from the sun below the horizon

when sunlight fades more stars appear
lending faint light to the earth

I stand centered on the darkened land
and the sky comes down to my feet

I turn, and at every turn
see the curvature of the earth

with morning dusk
surface features begin to show
and the horizon recedes

from the outer world

a simple wooden bridge
leading to the world of the hermit

a useful and necessary bridge
between traffic and quiet,
roadside and path

over the creek
to the hermitage –
little more than a hut

let it be summer

when it is time to seek my narrow bed
I'll visit the meadow kept open by grazing elk
where wild violets grow

I would wish to re-visit distant meadows too
and tidal ditches and rivers of grass
spartina in the marsh, eelgrass in the sea
～　　　　～　　　　～
the grassy meadow in the Oregon Cascades
where as a child I sat drawing
the tiny flowers blooming there

near the old logging road
where, fifteen years later,
I saw my first, lone shooting star
～　　　　～　　　　～
and after a few more years
the field in Montana
solid pink with shooting stars
～　　　　～　　　　～
the wild asparagus on the roadside
north out of Chicago where I meant to return
when it was time to harvest
～　　　　～　　　　～
the dry coast of Turkey
where a young girl gave me
all her small fist would hold
of wild, white narcissus
～　　　　～　　　　～

the St. Simons Island tidal ditch,
intoxicating with the aroma of ginger lilies,
where once I saw a Little Green Heron

～　　　～　　　～

it would take much time and travel to visit
all these and the other important places –
I shall visit them all in memory

But let it be summer in an elk-grazed meadow
on the Oregon coast and I shall be satisfied
to once again see a field of violets

frost and cold

blue sea

silence

"*I look at every thing* ('escape'). And indeed she does. With close, intense observations of the natural world, Shirley Plummer, using free verse form, gives her narrator a voice that moves from wistfulness, through a kind of baffled anger – this happens then that happens, but to what avail? – and into a generous embrace of life's difficulties and of aging. Noting changes in weather, in the moods of sky and sea, even switching views by shifting from one small window to another, *the task of falling rain* traces developments inside the poet's own mind and spirit, almost as if each dutifully named plant, creature, phenomenon were direct agency for long ago losses and present pains. A remarkable, haunting debut collection. Anyone who loves the sea will want to keep it close."

–Jean Esteve, author of *Winter Sun* and *Off-Key*, an Oregon Book Award finalist in poetry

"In her first full-length collection, Shirley Plummer honors the complex, mutable beauty of the Oregon coastal terrain she loves. Her marvelous names for rain – lavish rain, lullaby rain, tattoo and gravid and spendthrift rain – could just as aptly convey some of the overall range and depth she achieves in her work. In *the task of falling rain*, Plummer's poems take on an admirable endeavor: to embrace her home's flora and fauna, to celebrate whatever rain touches and feeds."

– Paulann Petersen, Oregon Poet Laureate Emerita

"*We keep a diary to know each possibility probed / and those that have yet to be explored / to find where the lion lives / and if the coyotes hang out in that cave*, writes Shirley Plummer, in a beautiful first collection by a seasoned poet who lives in a temperate rainforest on the edge of the Pacific Ocean in Oregon. Plummer carefully examines life with a microscopic eye, revealing the power of the natural world. *The sea*, she writes in this long-awaited debut collection, *is always in my senses*. And now, too, with this book, it is in ours."

– Drew Myron, author of *Thin Skin: Poems & Photos*

Shirley Plummer is a native of Oregon, born, raised and schooled in Salem in the Willamette Valley. In her mid-school years parts of summer holidays were spent in the Cascades, where she found a "home" in the forest. Later she felt an exile, and decades of moving house and traveling did not lessen her wish to return. The painful death of her beloved freed her to do so.

She now lives on the central Oregon coast between the Siuslaw National Forest and the Pacific Ocean near her three children. Her older sister still lives in Salem. In 2011 her notebook declares, "I am a poet and this is my year," and editors began accepting her work. This volume is her first collection.

www.ingramcontent.com/pod-product-compliance
Lightning Source LLC
Chambersburg PA
CBHW042331150426
43194CB00001B/20